IN DISGUISE ON THE UNDERGROUND RAILROAD

A GRAPHIC NOVEL BIOGRAPHY OF
ANNA MARIA WEEMS

WRITTEN BY MYRA FAYE TURNER   ILLUSTRATED BY MARKIA JENAI

Published by Capstone Press, an imprint of Capstone
1710 Roe Crest Drive, North Mankato, Minnesota 56003
capstonepub.com

Library of Congress Cataloging-in-Publication Data
Names: Turner, Myra Faye, author. | Jenai, Markia, illustrator.
Title: In disguise on the underground railroad : a graphic novel biography of Anna
Maria Weems / by Myra Faye Turner ; illustrated by Markia Jenai.
Description: North Mankato, Minnesota : Capstone Press, [2024] | Series: Barrier
breakers | Includes bibliographical references. | Audience: Ages 8-11 | Audience:
Grades 4-6 | Summary: "Anna Maria Weems was just a teenager when she was
given the opportunity to escape her enslaver in the mid-1800s. The journey would
be dangerous, but she would have the help of abolitionists along the way. One
of those supporters had a novel idea—Anna Maria would escape to freedom
disguised as a boy. Learn about her brave journey on the Underground Railroad in
this inspiring graphic novel."— Provided by publisher.
Identifiers: LCCN 2023019031 (print) | LCCN 2023019032 (ebook) | ISBN
9781669061748 (hardcover) | ISBN 9781669061823 (paperback) | ISBN
9781669061786 (pdf) | ISBN 9781669061847 (kindle edition) | ISBN 9781669061830
(epub)
Subjects: LCSH: Weems, Anne-Marie—Juvenile literature. | Weems, Anne-Marie—
Comic books, strips, etc. | Fugitive slaves—United States—Biography—Juvenile
literature. | Fugitive slaves—United States—Biography—Comic books, strips, etc.
| Underground Railroad—Juvenile literature. | Underground Railroad—Comic
books, strips, etc. | LCGFT: Biographical comics. | Educational comics. | Graphic
novels.
Classification: LCC E450.W39 T87 2024 (print) | LCC E450.W39 (ebook) |
DDC 973.7/115092 [B]—dc23/eng/20230512
LC record available at https://lccn.loc.gov/2023019031
LC ebook record available at https://lccn.loc.gov/2023019032

Editorial Credits
Editor: Julie Gassman; Designer: Dina Her; Production Specialist: Tori Abraham

Image Credit
Wikimedia: Public Domain, 28

Printed and bound in the USA. 5626

TABLE OF CONTENTS

Longing for Freedom

Enslaved people first arrived in the Americas from Africa in the 1600s. They did not come willingly. Instead, they were kidnapped and shipped across the wide blue ocean. When they arrived, the Africans were sold to white enslavers.

Ten to 12 million Africans were brought to the Americas and enslaved. Enslaved people longed for freedom.

One day we'll be free.

Then we can work for ourselves.

Many gained freedom before the United States government abolished slavery in 1865. Some were freed by their enslaver. Others had their freedom purchased by family or friends. Some enslaved people took matters into their own hands. They escaped.

John Weems was free, but his wife, Arrah, was enslaved. Because of laws at the time, this meant their children were enslaved at birth. Around 1840, the couple welcomed a new baby girl.

What should we call her?

Let's name her Anna Maria.

John Weems worked hard to keep his family together. The couple and their eight children lived in Rockville, Maryland. John made yearly payments to his family's enslaver, Adam Robb, so that all the Weems could live together.

As long as you keep paying me, I promise I won't sell your family.

I'm saving as much as I can, so we can all be free.

I know you're doing the best you can, John.

Robb had also promised to one day sell the family to John if he could get enough money. But saving money was hard. Then, in 1847, tragedy struck. Life for the Weems family was forever changed.

A Family Torn Apart

In 1847, Robb died suddenly. His death left the Weems family worried about their future.

Papa, what's gonna happen to us?

Don't worry, Anna. Everything's going to be okay.

While Robb's estate was being settled, John immediately began trying to raise money to buy his family's freedom before they could be sold and possibly moved down South.

Mr. Robb promised me we could stay together. I hope his family will make the same promise.

I hope so too. I don't know what I would do without you and the children.

Unfortunately, that was not the case. In December 1849, Robb's daughter sold Arrah and the children to pay off debts. The family was torn apart.

I beg you, please wait for my husband to return.

Mama, don't let them take me!

Anna, along with her sister Catherine, were sold to Charles Price. Price owned a tavern and several farms in Unity, Maryland.

Catherine, I miss Mama and Papa.

Me too. But we have each other. And Papa will come for us.

Arrah and the boys were sold down South. In 1850, the third Weems daughter, Mary Jane, escaped with her uncle and aunt to the free state of New York.

John traveled to New York City, hoping to get money from Mary Jane. However, she was no longer in the north.

All wasn't lost though. Supporters set up the Weems Ransom Fund, to help the father bring his family back home. He also had help from lawyer Jacob Bigelow. Bigelow acted on the family's behalf for the return of John's wife and children.

I hope my chance at freedom comes soon.

In 1853, Catherine, Arrah, and the two youngest Weems boys were emancipated. This left Anna and three of her brothers still enslaved.

Price repeatedly refused to sell Anna back to her family. Most likely he was holding out for more money from her rescuers or from another enslaver.

Price watched Anna closely. He even made her sleep in his bedroom with him and his wife. But in time, he let Anna return to her own room. He figured her friends had given up any plans to help her escape.

No, Anna will remain with me.

You better keep your eye on her. One day you might call for her and she won't answer.

Tonight, you can start sleeping in your own room again.

I'm so glad I can return to my room.

Around this time, Price actually moved closer to Anna's newly freed family. The Weems were now living in Washington, D.C. Price moved to Rockville and opened another tavern.

Did my family forget about me? I pray they will come for me one day soon.

The teen was so close to her parents. But she might as well have been on the other side of the world. So close, and yet unable to see or talk to them. The years were passing, but Anna still longed for freedom.

Anna's family hadn't forgotten about her. Neither had Jacob Bigelow and other allies. However, freeing an enslaved person sometimes took weeks or months. And in Anna's case, years. There was a lot of planning involved. And everything was done in secret.

Word of an escape plan for Anna, spread from mouth to ear.

Finally, the whispered words reached Anna's ear.

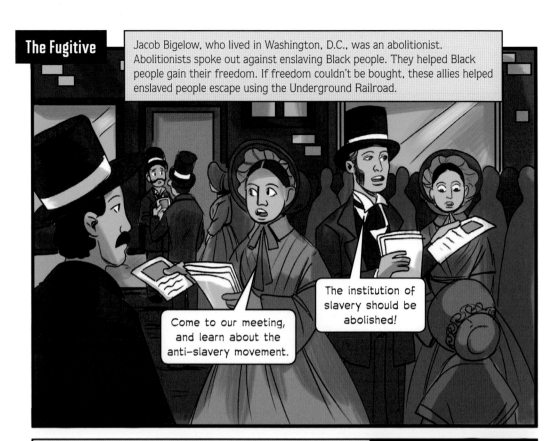

Jacob Bigelow, who lived in Washington, D.C., was an abolitionist. Abolitionists spoke out against enslaving Black people. They helped Black people gain their freedom. If freedom couldn't be bought, these allies helped enslaved people escape using the Underground Railroad.

The Underground Railroad wasn't a physical railroad. It was a secret network of Black and white abolitionists. "Conductors" helped enslaved people escape to free states in the north or to Canada.

Along with Bigelow, William Still developed the plan to help Anna escape. Still was part of a network of abolitionists in Philadelphia, Pennsylvania. The group was called the Philadelphia Vigilance Committee.

Still and Bigelow decided the best choice was for Anna to escape to Canada. She had an aunt and uncle living there.

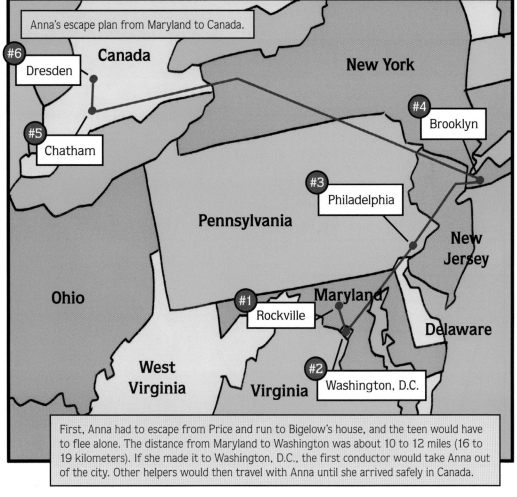

Anna's escape plan from Maryland to Canada.

Canada

New York

#6 Dresden

#4 Brooklyn

#5 Chatham

#3 Philadelphia

Pennsylvania

New Jersey

Ohio

#1 Rockville

Maryland

Delaware

West Virginia

Virginia

#2 Washington, D.C.

First, Anna had to escape from Price and run to Bigelow's house, and the teen would have to flee alone. The distance from Maryland to Washington was about 10 to 12 miles (16 to 19 kilometers). If she made it to Washington, D.C., the first conductor would take Anna out of the city. Other helpers would then travel with Anna until she arrived safely in Canada.

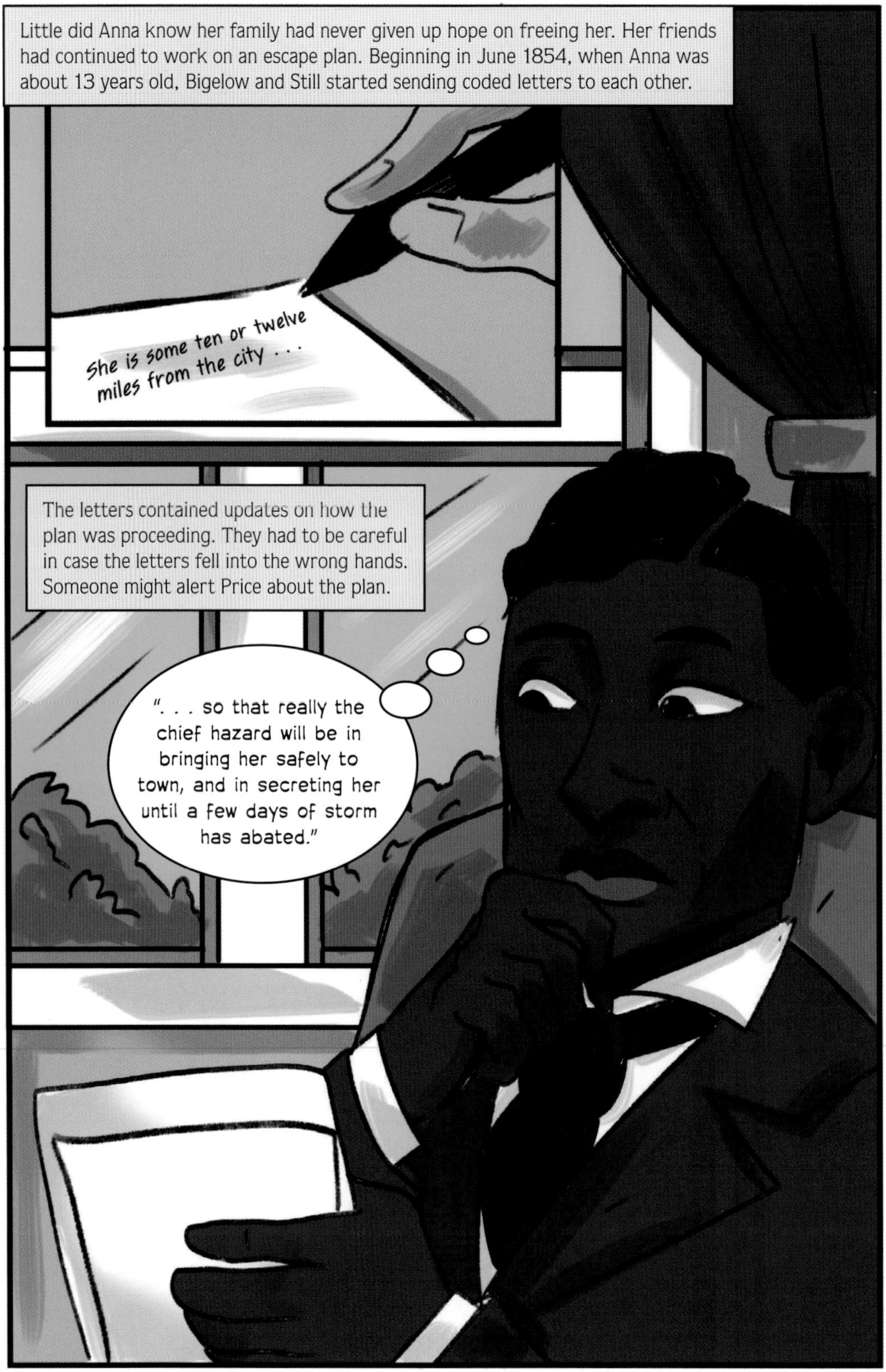
Little did Anna know her family had never given up hope on freeing her. Her friends had continued to work on an escape plan. Beginning in June 1854, when Anna was about 13 years old, Bigelow and Still started sending coded letters to each other.
She is some ten or twelve miles from the city . . .
The letters contained updates on how the plan was proceeding. They had to be careful in case the letters fell into the wrong hands. Someone might alert Price about the plan.
". . . so that really the chief hazard will be in bringing her safely to town, and in secreting her until a few days of storm has abated."

After those first whispered words, Anna was excited as she waited. But she had to act normal while she waited for the signal to run.

One day soon, I won't have to do chores for anyone but my family.

Anna was patient as she waited for weeks and then months. Finally, after waiting over a year, she received the words she had so longed to hear.

Tonight's the night. I can hardly wait!

September 23, 1855

Anna, now 15 years old, hurried to her quarters after finishing her chores.

When everything was quiet, Anna carefully slipped from her shabby cabin. She ran into the dark woods.

Anna ran for miles and miles through the black night. She waded through cool streams. She didn't dare look back.

This will throw off my scent when the hound dogs are looking for me.

Anna was breathless when she finally reached Jacob Bigelow's apartment in Washington, D.C.

Whew! I'm so glad I made it. I was scared I might get caught.

It feels good to be free.

She had completed the first leg of her journey to freedom.

You must be starving child. Would you like some more?

Yes please.

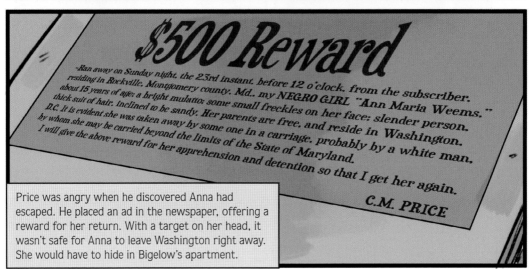

$500 Reward

–Ran away on Sunday night, the 23rd instant, before 12 o'clock, from the subscriber, residing in Rockville, Montgomery county, Md., my NEGRO GIRL "Ann Maria Weems," about 15 years of age: a bright mulatto; some small freckles on her face; slender person, thick suit of hair, inclined to be sandy. Her parents are free, and reside in Washington, D.C. It is evident she was taken away by some one in a carriage, probably by a white man, by whom she may be carried beyond the limits of the State of Maryland.

I will give the above reward for her apprehension and detention so that I get her again.

C.M. PRICE

Price was angry when he discovered Anna had escaped. He placed an ad in the newspaper, offering a reward for her return. With a target on her head, it wasn't safe for Anna to leave Washington right away. She would have to hide in Bigelow's apartment.

Since the slave hunters were looking for a girl, Bigelow came up with a novel idea. Anna would become Joe Wright, a male carriage driver.

I think this idea will work.

But sir, I don't know how to act like a boy.

Don't worry. I'll teach you. Hopefully, it will be safe for you to leave soon.

With Bigelow's help, Anna transformed into Joe. She wore boys' clothes.

She tucked her long hair under a boy's hat.

And she learned how to walk and carry herself like a boy.

You're doing great!

Yes, I think I got it sir.

Days turned into weeks—eight long weeks.

We think it's safe for you to leave now. I won't be going with you, though.

Who's going with me? I'm not going alone, am I?

No, Anna. We have friends who will help you. The first helper is Dr. Ellwood Harvey. He will take you out of the city.

It was decided the perfect meeting spot for Anna's escape was right in front of the White House! "Joe" and Bigelow met Dr. Harvey at the agreed-upon time.

Joe jumped into the driver's seat as the two men said their goodbyes.

Drive on.

Yes, doctor.

Anna drove the carriage for a while. Then Dr. Harvey took over. He would drive the rest of the way to the next stop—William Still's house in Philadelphia. The next leg of Anna's journey to true freedom had finally begun.

Pull over and let me drive. I want to be ready in case we run into any problems.

Yes, sir.

CLIPPITY CLOP

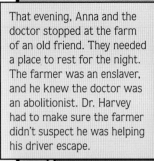

That evening, Anna and the doctor stopped at the farm of an old friend. They needed a place to rest for the night. The farmer was an enslaver, and he knew the doctor was an abolitionist. Dr. Harvey had to make sure the farmer didn't suspect he was helping his driver escape.

I assure you; I'm no longer involved in that sort of thing.

That's good, my old friend.

My health has been poor lately. I thought a drive through the countryside would help.

You're welcome here any time.

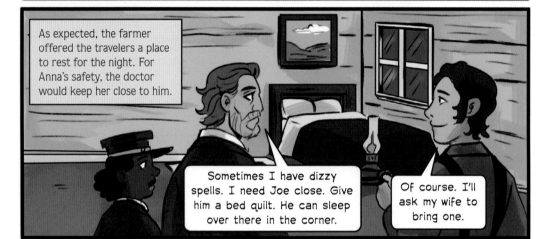

As expected, the farmer offered the travelers a place to rest for the night. For Anna's safety, the doctor would keep her close to him.

Sometimes I have dizzy spells. I need Joe close. Give him a bed quilt. He can sleep over there in the corner.

Of course. I'll ask my wife to bring one.

Early the next morning, Anna and Dr. Harvey left the farm. On Thanksgiving Day, November 22, nearly two months after Anna escaped from Price, they arrived at Still's house. Still's wife greeted the doctor.

My husband's not home at the moment.

I wish to leave this young lad with you a short while.

Dr. Harvey got back into the carriage and drove off. Mrs. Still wouldn't find out the lad was a teenage girl until later.

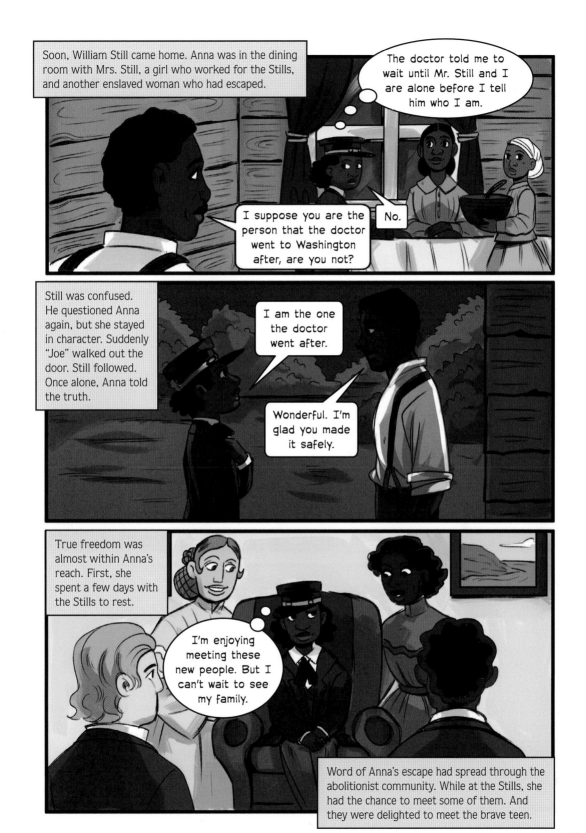

Soon, William Still came home. Anna was in the dining room with Mrs. Still, a girl who worked for the Stills, and another enslaved woman who had escaped.

The doctor told me to wait until Mr. Still and I are alone before I tell him who I am.

I suppose you are the person that the doctor went to Washington after, are you not?

No.

Still was confused. He questioned Anna again, but she stayed in character. Suddenly "Joe" walked out the door. Still followed. Once alone, Anna told the truth.

I am the one the doctor went after.

Wonderful. I'm glad you made it safely.

True freedom was almost within Anna's reach. First, she spent a few days with the Stills to rest.

I'm enjoying meeting these new people. But I can't wait to see my family.

Word of Anna's escape had spread through the abolitionist community. While at the Stills, she had the chance to meet some of them. And they were delighted to meet the brave teen.

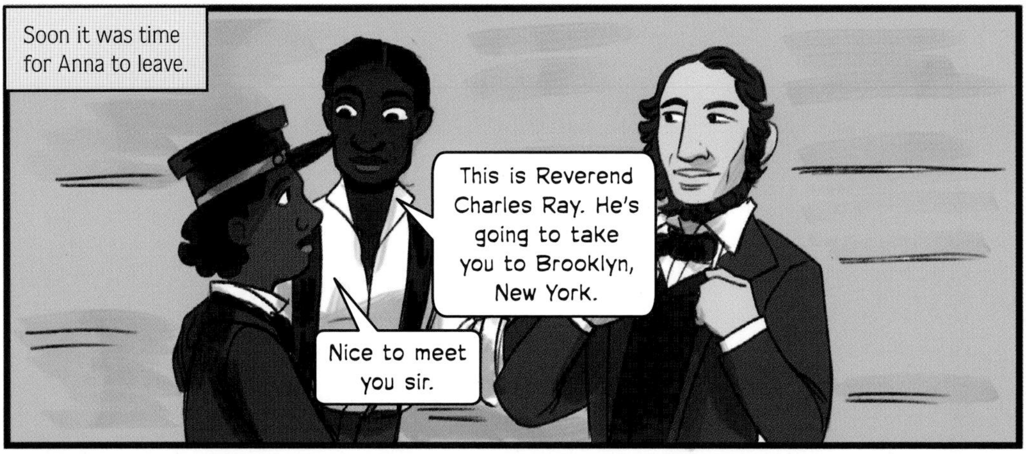
Soon it was time for Anna to leave.
This is Reverend Charles Ray. He's going to take you to Brooklyn, New York.
Nice to meet you sir.

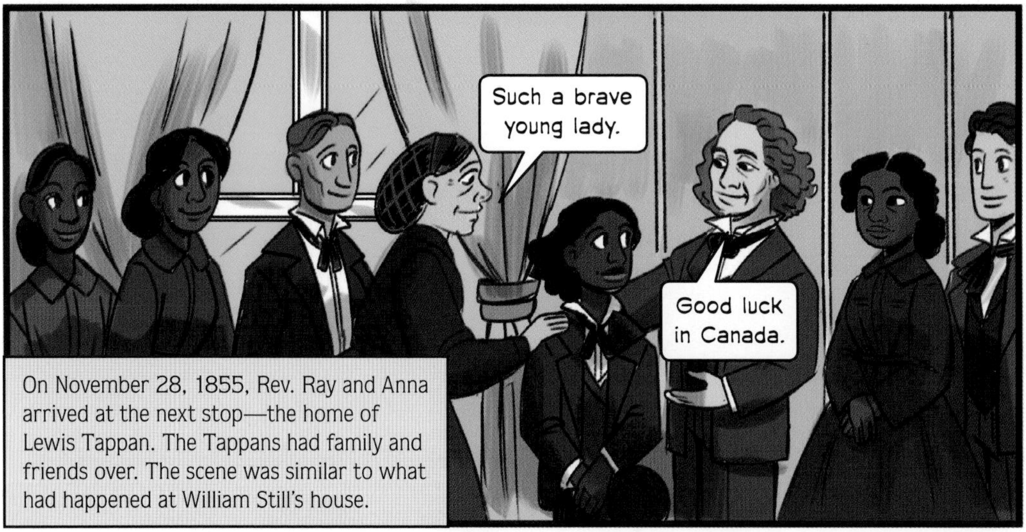
Such a brave young lady.
Good luck in Canada.
On November 28, 1855, Rev. Ray and Anna arrived at the next stop—the home of Lewis Tappan. The Tappans had family and friends over. The scene was similar to what had happened at William Still's house.

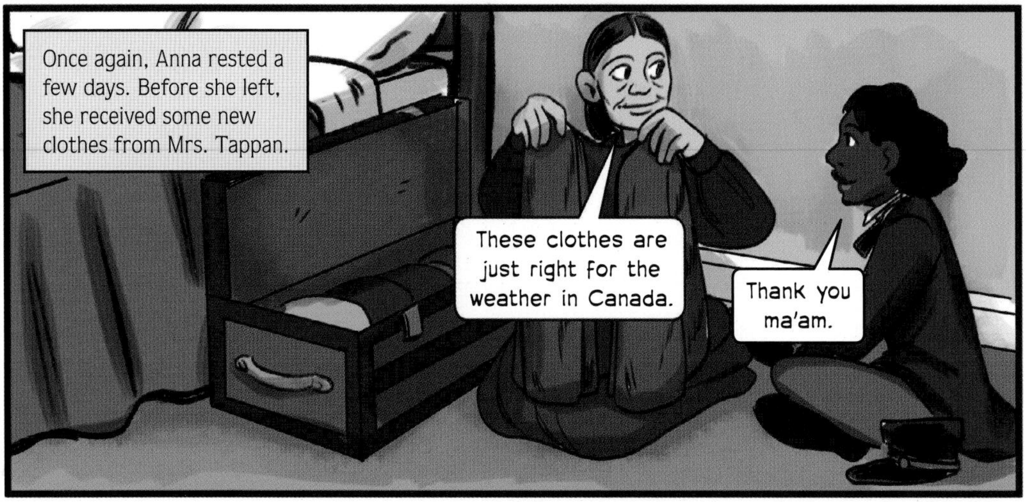
Once again, Anna rested a few days. Before she left, she received some new clothes from Mrs. Tappan.
These clothes are just right for the weather in Canada.
Thank you ma'am.

Friday, November 30, 1855

It was time for the last leg of Anna's journey. She had a new conductor, Rev. Amos Freeman.

Anna and Freeman worried someone might figure out Anna's identity. Freeman also wondered how the train would get over the Niagara Falls River and into Canada.

But no one seemed suspicious. And the conductor answered Freeman's question soon enough.

Next stop, Canada. Are you ready?

Yes! I'm so happy to be free. I miss my mama and papa and my sisters and brothers. But I have my aunt and uncle.

Please stay seated while the train goes across the bridge.

At last Anna set foot on free soil. She wanted to jump for joy at her newfound freedom. But Anna was still nervous and unsure of how to behave.

It's okay, child. You're free. You can relax now.

I prayed for this day for so long. Thank you.

They were in Chatham, a town in Ontario, Canada. Chatham is about 200 miles (322 km) from where they crossed the border.

Can I see my uncle and aunt now?

Not yet. We have about 16 miles before we reach their farm.

Are you looking for a place to stay?

Can I rent a wagon? We're trying to get to Dresden tonight.

No. It's dark outside and the roads are too muddy.

Then yes, I guess we need a place to stay.

The man took the travelers to his boarding house. They joined a few other guests in the parlor. Chatham was a refuge for formerly enslaved people. So, Rev. Freeman felt it was safe to reveal Anna's identity.

Can I speak to you in private?

That young man is a female. She escaped from Washington dressed like that. I would like her to change her clothes now.

I can't believe it! I'll have my wife help her.

Let's turn you back into a lovely young woman.

I'm ready.

I'm pleased to introduce you to Miss Anna Maria Weems!

On Monday, December 3, Rev. Freeman and Anna set out for her uncle and aunt's farm. Unbeknownst to them, they met Anna's uncle on the way.

Can you tell me how far it is to the Bradley farm?

About a mile.

Anna's uncle was cautious. He wasn't sure who this stranger was. He started giving directions to the farm. Then he stopped and told them the truth.

I suppose I'm the one you're looking for. My name's Bradley.

For the first time, the farmer noticed the young girl sitting quietly in the wagon.

Anna Maria, child is that you?

Yes, uncle, it's me!

We never expected to see you again! Your aunt will be so happy you're here.

That evening, Anna celebrated her newfound freedom with family. The Bradleys also asked about the loved ones they left behind. But most of all, they were happy to have Anna with them.

Anna had traveled by foot, carriage, and train to reach her final destination. She had six fearless Underground Railroad conductors to assist in her journey. Many other helpers also aided the teen's flight Anna had traveled over 500 miles (805 km) from Rockville to Canada. The journey took over two months. But at last, for the first time in Anna's life, she went to sleep truly free.

Not much is known about Anna's life after she settled in Canada. However, Canada was home to many Black people who fled their oppressors. They created lives and new communities of Black Canadians. Many of the descendants of those first settlers still live in Canada today.

It's believed Anna was educated at the Buxton Mission School. Buxton was a settlement established for Black Canadians.

Little else is known about the brave teen, including the date and place of her death. Still, Anna's triumph over her circumstances is inspiring.

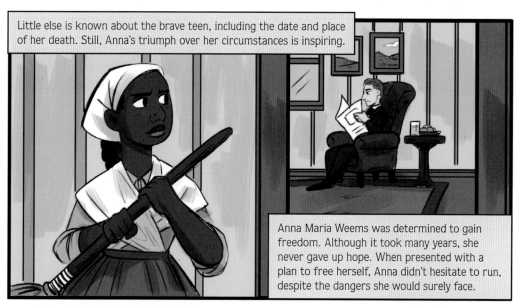

Anna Maria Weems was determined to gain freedom. Although it took many years, she never gave up hope. When presented with a plan to free herself, Anna didn't hesitate to run, despite the dangers she would surely face.

Anna's story is also a rare look inside the Underground Railroad. The network operated in secret. This was to keep both themselves and escapees safe.

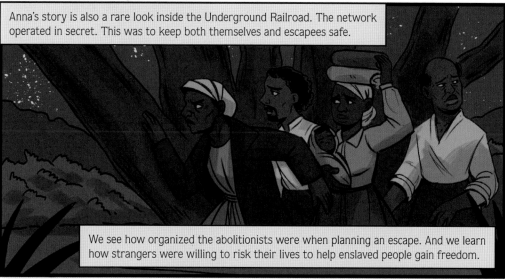

We see how organized the abolitionists were when planning an escape. And we learn how strangers were willing to risk their lives to help enslaved people gain freedom.

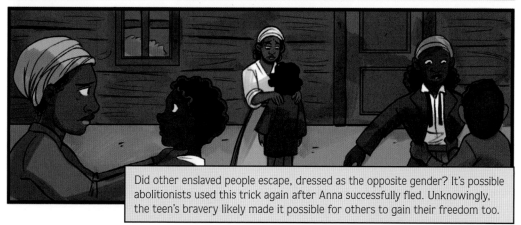

Did other enslaved people escape, dressed as the opposite gender? It's possible abolitionists used this trick again after Anna successfully fled. Unknowingly, the teen's bravery likely made it possible for others to gain their freedom too.

MORE ABOUT ANNA MARIA WEEMS

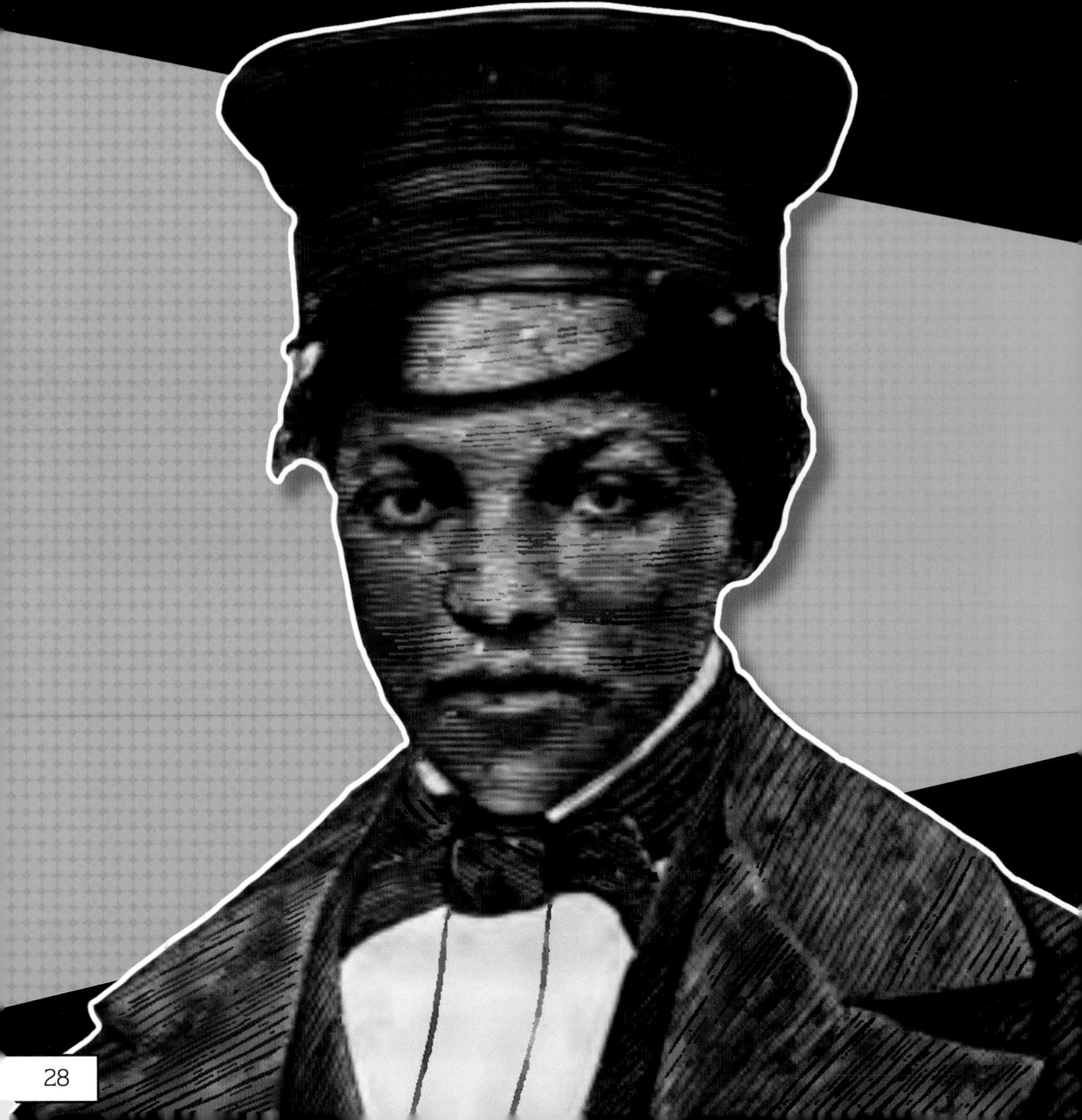

- Anna was also referred to as Ann Maria Weems.

- Anna's mother was also called "Arabella" or "Airy."

- By 1853, the Weems Family Fund had raised $5,000 to free the remaining enslaved children.

- After Anna escaped, her three brothers remained enslaved in Alabama. It wasn't until 1858 that the last brother's freedom was purchased.

- Bigelow and Still considered having Anna's mother or her two cousins escort her north. But they decided it would be too risky for the adults.

GLOSSARY

abolish (uh-BOL-ish)—to put an end to

abolitionist (ab-uh-LISH-uh-nist)—a person who advocated for the ending of slavery in the United States

ally (AL-eye)—a person who provides help and support to another

boarding house (bohr-ding HOUS)—a house where people rent rooms from the owner

debt (DET)—something that is owed to another

network (NET-wurk)—a group of interconnected people

oppressive (uh-PRES-iv)—harsh or unjust

ransom (RAN-suhm)—money paid to release someone held against their will

suspicious (suh-SPISH-uhs)—to suspect or distrust

tavern (TAV-ern)—an inn or place for travelers to rest, eat, etc.

READ MORE

Enz, Tammy. *Science on the Underground Railroad*. North Mankato, MN: Capstone Press, 2023.

Wilkins, Ebony Joy. *If You Traveled on the Underground Railroad*. New York: Scholastic Press, 2022.

Williams, Carla. *The Underground Railroad*. Mankato, MN: The Child's World, 2021.

INTERNET SITES

The Underground Railroad
kids.nationalgeographic.com/history/article/the-underground-railroad

Escape to Freedom
sn2.scholastic.com/issues/2019-20/030220.html

Henry "Box" Brown
kids.britannica.com/students/article/Henry-Box-Brown/631819

ABOUT THE AUTHOR

Myra Faye Turner is a New Orleans-based poet and author. She has written for grownups, but prefers writing for young readers. She has written two dozen nonfiction books for children and young adults, covering diverse topics like politics, the Apollo moon landing, edible insects, and U.S. history. When she's not writing, she spends her days reading, napping, and drinking coffee.

ABOUT THE ILLUSTRATOR

Markia Jenai was raised in Detroit, Michigan, during rough times but found adventure through art, drawing, and storytelling. Those interests led her to study at the Academy of Art University in San Francisco, California. An avid lover of fantasy settings, cultures, and mythology, Markia has made it her goal to create worlds where people of color are front and center. Diversity within her art means the world to her, and she dreams of the day when everyone will see themselves in media and have the same access to telling their own stories.